COMBATTING SHAMING
and Toxic Communities™

COMBATTING

DISCRIMINATION AGAINST WOMEN IN THE GAMER COMMUNITY

MARTY GITLIN

ROSEN
PUBLISHING®

New York

Published in 2017 by The Rosen Publishing Group, Inc.
29 East 21st Street, New York, NY 10010

Library of Congress Cataloging-in-Publication Data

Names: Gitlin, Marty, author.
Title: Combatting discrimination against women in the gamer community / Marty Gitlin.
Description: New York : Rosen Publishing, 2017. | Series: Combatting shaming and toxic communities | Audience: Grades 7–12. | Includes bibliographical references and index.
Identifiers: LCCN 2015051393 | ISBN 978-1-5081-7118-8 (library bound)
Subjects: LCSH: Sex discrimination against women—Juvenile literature. | Sex crimes—Juvenile literature.
Classification: LCC HQ1237 .G558 2016 | DDC 305.42—dc23
LC record available at http://lccn.loc.gov/2015051393

Manufactured in China

CONTENTS

INTRODUCTION

Zoe Quinn was just a little girl when a family friend presented her with a Game Boy. The gift made her one of the happiest kids in her tiny town in upstate New York. It inspired her to dart about the woods and play the role of Samus Aran, from the game *Metroid*. Zoe pretended the sticks she carried were swords with which she attacked imaginary aliens.

Her love affair with gaming had begun. It nourished her imagination and cultivated her creativity. She eventually yearned to embark on a career that would allow her to embrace her passion, but she had nothing specific in mind. She wrote science fiction stories. She became quite adept at taking pictures.

Then, a bad break turned into a good one. Quinn was offered a job as a photographer in Toronto. But upon her arrival, the position was no longer available. Rather than return to the United States, she stayed in the city to meet indie game developers.

Quinn was hooked. She decided that game development was her future. She eventually began designing silly comedy games such as *Realistic Relationship Simulator*, in which players were forced to decide whether or not to expel gas in front of their dates.

Soon Quinn created an interactive novel called *Depression Quest*, which was inspired by her own struggles with the condition. Released as a browser game in February 2013, it quickly gained popularity and media attention. She placed it on

Greenlight, a community review section of the gaming download site Steam.

All was well—but not for long. Some on Steam considered Quinn an outsider. She began receiving menacing phone calls and even rape threats. One email delivered the hope of her suicide. She withdrew the game from Steam but refused to be defeated and soon resubmitted it. The hate continued. And that was the least of her problems.

In August 2014, Quinn's ex-boyfriend Eron Gjoni uploaded a blog post claiming that Quinn had cheated on him with games writer Nathan Grayson. Gjoni linked the blog with Internet chat site 4Chan, which is popular with gamers. Quinn believed Gjoni wanted to ruin her life.

He nearly succeeded. Gamers began "doxxing" Quinn, posting her contact details and personal photos on social media. Posters alleged that she had slept with Grayson in order to convince him to write a positive review of *Depression Quest*. Actor Adam Baldwin tweeted his support of the accusers, using the hashtag #GamerGate. The catchy moniker caught on. GamerGate had begun.

Quinn realizes that issues regarding antiwomen sentiment in gaming extend far beyond her struggles. The depiction of women as sex objects and the sexual violence perpetrated against them in games is an issue. How women have been treated within the gaming industry is an issue. The treatment of women in the burgeoning social media among gamers is an issue. The question is, how can it all be stopped?

WHAT'S AT STAKE

It was August 25, 2014. Media critic Anita Sarkeesian released a video as part of her Feminist Frequency series titled *Tropes vs. Women*, in which she examines the representation of women in popular games such as *Call of Duty*, *Grand Theft Auto*, and *Hitman*.

Sarkeesian was pointing out nothing new. Many critics and even some fans of those games had objected to the sexual violence against women depicted in those titles. They also cited the senseless slaughter that many believe has played a role in the increase in real-life violence and even murder in American society. Yet even some who railed against the violence maintained an attraction to those games as a guilty pleasure.

Therein lies one of the most significant problems. Rather than boycotting games that promote violence against women, many of those who are aware of the issue continue to play them. One of the first steps toward change must come from male and female gamers who take a stand by not purchasing products that feature blatantly sexual depictions of women and violence against them.

Decreased sales motivate developers to stop creating games that objectify women. However, too many gamers have continued

Media critic and Feminist Frequency founder Anita Sarkeesian has taken a lead in improving depictions of women in video games.

to play them—despite understanding their negative impact—simply because they consider them fun.

The Sarkeesian haters exploded upon the posting of her video. They offered their skewed view that feminists in the media were acting as censors of games rather than objective reviewers. GamerGate, which began as an attack on developer Zoe Quinn, intensified. Now it targeted all those who railed against discrimination against women in the gaming industry and the objectification of women within the games themselves.

Sarkeesian was forced to flee her home and could no longer appear at gaming events without receiving death threats. Online forums continued to be peppered with posts spewing hate against all those who decried the negative portrayal of women in video games and the treatment of women within the industry.

The haters seemed to be embracing their contribution to the harm caused to such women as Quinn and Sarkeesian.

The paranoid charge was that a clique of feminists was conspiring to take over the gaming industry. The GamerGate backers made their claims under the guise of anti-censorship and journalistic ethics. And game producers were listening. They did not want to alienate their fans. Their silence allowed the haters to escalate the war of words. The harassment worsened. Someone even sent naked pictures of Quinn to her father.

Sarkeesian and Quinn were not the lone targets. Another

victim was Brianna Wu, who cofounded the independent game development company Giant Spacekat. She, too, was forced out of her Boston home after receiving rape and death threats from GamerGate supporters following her creation of a highly successful action game called *Revolution 60*, which was targeted to a female playing audience. More than 250,000 people downloaded the free version upon its release in July 2014. Its sales rate jumped to four times the national average.

Software engineer and Giant Spacekat cofounder Brianna Wu has fought back against personal threats and online abuse of females through positivity and educational interaction.

NOTHING NEW FOR WU

Brianna Wu received so many rape threats after voicing opposition to Internet haters during the GamerGate controversy that she stopped reporting them.

The cofounder of Giant Spacekat, who has impacted the gaming industry through her development of games representing women in a positive way, has been confronted often by young girls who express fear in regard to pursuing a career in the business. She gives them no assurances, but she does not suggest they shy away either.

Wu told VentureBeat that she struggles with the issue every day. She empathizes with girls who yearn to get into the field because she experienced the same desires as a child in the 1980s. She receives letters or inquiries in person from girls ages eight to twelve who are afraid that they will receive the same level of abuse that Wu has been forced to deal with. "I look them in the eye and I promise that we'll make it better," Wu said. "We're following through on that."

The persecution of Wu extended beyond threats of violence to steps taken to ruin her career. Haters set up fake accounts to impersonate her online. They then faked quotes from her spewing out horrible insults against others in an attempt to wreck her professional reputation. She complained in an interview with PBS.org that it was the worst experience in her life and that she was actually forced to get the FBI and local police involved to track down the perpetrators.

Nothing seemed to help. The Internet trolls continued to terrorize Wu and her friends. But during her weekly podcast, she expressed her understanding that the sentiments against her and other gaming professionals such as Sarkeesian and Quinn are the product of a larger societal problem.

"You cannot have thirty years of portraying women as bimbos, sex objects, second bananas, cleavage-y eye candy," Wu said. "Eventually it normalizes this treatment of women. And I think something is really sick and broken in our culture."

Oh Man!

What has been broken within the industry is that game designers are almost exclu- sively male. Research by the Entertainment Software

This photo shows a man playing *Grand Theft Auto*, one of the most popular games of its era, but also one of the most dangerous with regard to objectification of women.

Association in 2014 revealed that 48 percent of all gamers are female, but a survey taken by the International Game Developers Association showed that just 21 percent of all game designers are women. An earlier study had the latter figure at just 11 percent and added that women in the industry earned 23 percent less than their male counterparts.

There are three major roadblocks to ending the dangerous portrayals of women in video games and discrimination against them in the companies that create those games.

Video game developers such as those shown in this photo working for the British company Jagex Game Studio have been mostly men for many years, but the tide has begun to turn.

One is that there simply aren't enough women in the business who feel safe enough in their jobs to stand up for peers such as Quinn and Wu and to speak out against the continued creation of games that objectify women.

The second is that real change will only be achieved when a high percentage of men in the industry also take a stand against it.

The third is that gamers who agree that there is a problem must gather the inner strength to stop purchasing games from companies that have been linked with discrimination against female employees and from those that continue to produce games featuring sexist portrayals of women.

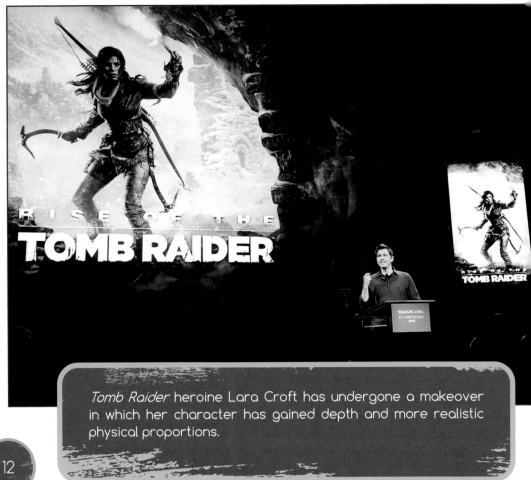

Tomb Raider heroine Lara Croft has undergone a makeover in which her character has gained depth and more realistic physical proportions.

Like many changes in the business world, the wheels turn slowly. But awareness brings progress. One woman who has established herself among the top echelon in the gaming community is Kate Edwards, who serves as the executive director of the International Game Developers Association. She works with companies to discourage them from using racial or sexual stereotypes in their games.

Edwards expressed particular pride about the changes in game character Lara Croft, heroine of the *Tomb Raider* series. Croft once typified the sexist female stereotype with exaggerated breast size and unrealistic body shape. Edwards was happy to report in 2014 that the new Lara Croft was more emotionally complex and modestly proportioned. However, Edwards also admitted that such changes can be difficult for gamers to accept.

They are also difficult for the male-dominated gaming media to accept. Many writers and reviewers not only backed Gamer-Gate, but also took the lead in promoting the idea that video games should be left alone. They have claimed that complaints of discrimination against women within the industry and about female characterization in games themselves have been greatly exaggerated.

The result is that journalists who back GamerGate have taken action against peers who have tried to influence companies to change their treatment and portrayal of women. They even have organized mass e-mail campaigns asking major corporations to pull their paid ads from websites such as such as Polygon and Rock, Paper, Shotgun that have challenged the industry to improve in regard to representations of women and minorities in video games.

Those who have defended the likes of Quinn and Wu understand that far more is at stake than their well-being and the state of the gaming industry. Freedom of expression and equality are two concepts that are supposed to be embraced in the United States. If females cannot freely ply their trades as game developers and if women in general do not receive equal opportunities in a business with unlimited future potential, that reflects negatively on the country as a whole.

Those working to end the harassment, level the playing field between males and females in the gaming industry, and end the sexist representations of women in games themselves see the bigger picture. But they are hoping for more help from gamers. After all, the buying public has more power than any individual.

DAMSELS IN
DISTRESS

The drawings of people and images in early video games were crude. That has changed. The representation of many women were also crude. However, that hasn't changed.

Those holding Atari controllers to play *Custer's Revenge* in the early 1980s were part of a burgeoning problem. The game depicted the famous general George Custer dodging flying arrows. His goal was to reach the other side of the screen so he could have sex with a naked Native American woman that had been held captive. *Custer's Revenge* caused a furor in America, but the objectification of women would only grow along with the gaming industry.

Far more disturbing games were yet to come—and not just in the United States. In 2006, a developer in Japan released a video game titled *RapeLay* in which players scored points by molesting a mother and her two daughters. They also received opportunities to rape selected female characters, including young schoolgirls, in trains and other places. The game even landed on Amazon.com, and though it did not last long, the mere idea that it was on the market in the first place can certainly be considered troubling.

Highly popular video games have been hardly less distressing. Included is *Grand Theft Auto V*, the top-selling game of 2013, in which strippers and prostitutes play roles in the plot. The game has also drawn controversy as one of the most violent on the market. Then again, a report submitted by the Entertainment Software Association revealed that violent video games are the best sellers. Many of them feature scantily clad women as sex objects or the targets of violence.

One must not concede, however, that improved representation of women cannot go hand-in-hand with the thirst of gamers for violence. By the second decade of the twenty-first century, the industry had begun designing more games with powerful female characters. But the battle has just started. Angela Love, who serves as the chairperson of the media arts and animation faculty at the Art Institute of Pittsburgh, believes that the treatment of women as sex objects must be eliminated if they are to be featured as realistic protagonists in such games.

"You fight the culture clichés," Love told the *Pittsburgh Tribune-Review*. "If you're only going to clad your characters in a tank top and miniskirt, how's she going to fight in that?" Love stressed the importance of teaching students to design complex, story-driven games without demeaning women.

Such changes are needed, if previous studies are any indication. One conducted by the psychology department at Oklahoma State University in 2007 researched 225 video games obtained from online retail stores. It determined that male characters were four times more frequently portrayed in game action, yet their female counterparts were more likely to be objectified with exaggerated sexiness. It was further established

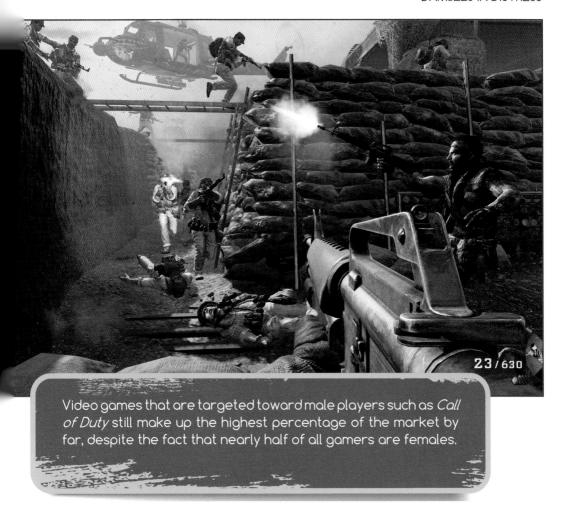

Video games that are targeted toward male players such as *Call of Duty* still make up the highest percentage of the market by far, despite the fact that nearly half of all gamers are females.

that violence and sexiness were paired more frequently with female characters. The study concluded that such portrayals could have a negative effect on gamers.

Shaping Young Minds

It has been argued that blatant sexual representations of women in gaming are more detrimental than in movies, on television, and online. This is because video games are played to a large extent by teenagers whose perceptions of gender

Young women still in the process of forming their identities are especially vulnerable to representations of women in media. A video game such as *Grand Theft Auto IV* does not offer positive role models for girls.

roles and identity are still being formed. Teenage boys influenced by the video games they play could establish a view of women as sex objects and potential targets of violence. Teenage girls who play the same games could view themselves as less intelligent and judged more by outside appearance than inner beauty and talent.

Nobody claims that every young person is damaged by playing video games that objectify women. Those with positive female figures in their lives that have a greater influence on them than any game could might certainly be unaffected. But such is not always the case. Many critics of those games argue that they can play a psychological role in motivating young men to perform violent acts against women or permanently damage the self-images of young women.

Women in video games are most often sexual entities. They are portrayed as the weaker sex. They exist to be desired or rescued. Sarkeesian believes that, coupled with other examples of negative female representation in the media, such games can result in retarding healthy emotional growth of young people, as well as gender stereotyping by any gamer.

ANITA THE ADVOCATE

Media critic Anita Sarkeesian became heavily involved in writing about the gaming industry during the GamerGate controversy of 2014. It was not unfamiliar territory for her. After all, she is the creator of Feminist Frequency, a video series on the Internet that explores the representation of media in all of pop culture.

Sarkeesian has toiled to break down stereotypes of women while highlighting issues of harassment and intimidation of women online and in gaming. Her work has motivated her to give lectures and presentations at

(continued on the next page)

(continued from the previous page)

various conferences and game development events around the world. Her honesty resulted in death threats and other forms of intimidation from haters but also great respect from those in the industry.

In fact, her contributions to the gaming world earned her the 2013 honorary award from the National Academy of Video Game Trade Reviewers, the 2014 Microsoft Women in Games Ambassador Award, and the 2014 Game Developers Choice Ambassador Award.

"Engaging with these games is not going to magically transform players into raging sexists," Sarkeesian said in part two of a video titled *Damsels in Distress*. "However, media narratives have a powerful cultivation effect, helping to shape cultural attitudes and opinions. So when developers exploit sensationalized images of brutalized, mutilated, and victimized women over and over again, it tends to reinforce the dominant gender paradigm, which casts men as aggressive and commanding and frames women as subordinate and dependent."

The increasing number of female characters cast as heroes in recent years has resulted in more prideful roles for women in video games. But game designers and manufacturers have continued to present female protagonists as sex objects in both body shape and dress. More realistic characters such as the new Lara Croft remain few and far between. Most are designed based on what is believed male gamers want to see despite the fact that females now make up nearly half of the gaming population.

Those female gamers are not even provided the option of selecting a woman protagonist in the majority of mainstream games. It has been offered that, in regard to violent games in particular, a women hero would seem unrealistic. Many believe that is a dangerous stereotype, especially to young male and female players. Tough women, some among the criminal element (such as axe murderer Lizzie Borden and bank robber Bonnie Parker), abound in American history. Those claiming there should be more female protagonists believe they can be effectively portrayed in video games.

Calling All Women

The first step, however, would be to include more female pro-tagonists of any kind in video games. A 2012 study by Electronic Entertainment Design and Research of 669 games showed that only 24 featured female lead characters. And that angers Samantha Allen, who spoke about the disparity as a third-year doctoral student in the Department of Women's, Gender, and Sexuality Studies at Emory University.

"I'm sick of seeing the same white scruffy face in every single game," she complained. "Once that face was the face of gaming, but now women make up almost half of the people who play games. We're still waiting for game publishers to catch up to their audience…Publishers swear up and down that female-driven games won't sell. When they do 'take a chance' on a female protagonist, they don't back up the games with a sufficient marketing budget."

Research backs that assertion. Games with male heroes, according to one figure, sell 75 percent better than those with female counterparts. But the counterargument is that manufacturers promote such games far more aggressively. It has been stated that games featuring women receive 60 percent less

It has been suggested that domestic violence has been exacerbated by the gaming industry, which promotes violent games and the objectification of women.

of the marketing budget on average. They simply have not been given a fair chance.

Many women in the gamer community rail against violent games regardless of the hero's gender. They argue that such games, which make up a large percentage of all that are available on the market, promote real-life violence, much of which victimizes women.

One government analysis combined statistics of various studies and tested the effect of violent video games on aggressive behavior. It concluded that exposure to violent games brought about the risk of increased aggression and decreased empathy for others.

Though it also determined that both genders were equally susceptible to an increase in violent behavior, the National Coalition Against Domestic Violence reports that a woman is assaulted or beaten on the average of every nine seconds in the United States. That statistic suggests that females are more endangered by the effects of violent video games.

Other options in regard to female representation might seem more palatable. Nonviolent games abound, but the characterization

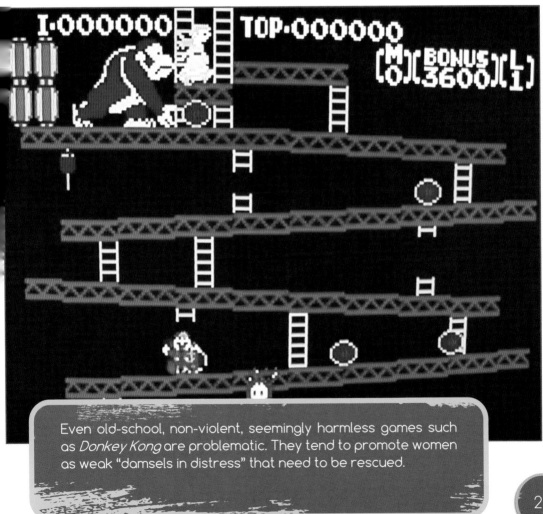

Even old-school, non-violent, seemingly harmless games such as *Donkey Kong* are problematic. They tend to promote women as weak "damsels in distress" that need to be rescued.

of women in most of those fall under the "damsel in distress" category. Even female characters in beloved, old-school games like *Super Mario Brothers* such as Princess and Peach are not only secondary to the title characters of Mario and Luigi, but they are also portrayed as weak and presented as caricatures of femininity, with their frilly pink dresses and abundance of jewelry.

The lack of strong female characters in nonviolent games and the negative stereotyping of the comparatively few women heroes in action games have remained concerning outside and inside the industry for many years.

Changes come slowly and carry risks to those who make their voices heard. However, boycotting games that feature negative representations of women, urging others to do the same, and expressing one's feelings to manufacturers through purchases and various forums can all make a difference.

As for women who work in the gaming business, they are taking action against negative stereotyping of female characters as well as their own mistreatment. That, too, is an uphill climb.

COMBATTING
MISTREATMENT

A poster on the online site *Kotaku*, a video game blog for Gawker Media, was fed up with complaints from women about their role in the gaming industry. So he wrote the following:

> I always wonder why women can't do anything but [complain] and moan. I mean, if you want video games for women and are as talented as your male developer colleagues, then just make one. Develop your own game...What is it with this massive entitlement? Video games are a male-dominated culture so naturally there will be mostly games targeted at males...If you want to have your own niche in the industry, then carve it out, don't expect other people to present it to you on a silver platter just because [you're a woman].

What most women and men in the business understand is that such claims are as full of holes as Swiss cheese. Women have

These teenage sisters are two of millions of girls that have narrowed the gender gap in regard to gaming—nearly half of all gamers are now female.

indeed developed their own games, but their underrepresentation in the development industry has resulted in comparatively few reaching the market and gaining popularity. Video gaming is not a male-dominated culture. Nearly half of all gamers are female. And women have not expected anything to be handed to them on a silver platter. They have simply asked for fairness and, in many cases, have received disrespect and discrimination instead.

One man who wanted answers was Luke Crane. Crane, a fantasy role-playing gamer and employee at Kickstarter, the world's largest funding platform for creative projects, asked a simple question in November 2012. He wondered why there were so few female game creators. The Twitter hashtag #onereasonwhy sprang up overnight, prompting replies from both women and men.

The response was overwhelming on both sides. Women revealed why they had grown disenchanted with the gaming industry while men revealed their thoughts through their answers. One woman claimed she had been told she would not be remembered by her own talents, but rather by the men it was presumed she had slept with. Another woman stated that she had been groped at conventions for game designers. Yet another overheard a male art manager say that he no longer hired women because "they're more trouble than they're worth."

Some of the men who answered Crane's question simply proved the point of their female counterparts by delivering the following message: If you can't handle the harassment, you're not worthy of being in the business. One wrote that if women are "too sensitive and self-absorbed to deal with criticism, it's

British author and video game writer Rhianna Pratchett seeks to encourage women to gain the courage to follow their dreams in the gaming industry despite obstacles.

good they don't design video games." Another compared the underrepresentation of women in the gaming industry to the lack of obese people teaching yoga.

British author and video game writer Rhianna Pratchett, who worked on such popular titles as *Tomb Raider*, *Rise of the Tomb Raider*, *Overlord*, and *Heavenly Sword*, responded by creating #onereasontobe, which invited women to explain why they wanted to enter or remain in the gaming industry.

The replies ranged from the desire to change the culture in favor of women to a simple passion for video games. One game developer indicated that the vast majority of men in the business brought her positive experiences. "For every [terrible] misogynist, there are loads of respectable, funny & brilliant men & women to work with," she wrote.

Indeed, the industry is changing. According to research done by the International Game Developers Association in 2014, the number of female developers had doubled over the previous five years from 11 percent to 22 percent. Although that represents progress, the percentage of women creating games remains woefully behind the percentage of female gamers.

Quite the Conundrum

The message is muddled. Women such as Pratchett, who are excited about their place in the gaming industry, might believe that the only permanent solution to female representation and the objectification of the gender in games is the continued increase in hiring. But on the other hand, the harassment, such as what was experienced during GamerGate, has driven women out of the business. The environment for women as game developers and in other related fields must be welcoming if the positive changes that have taken place are to continue.

Female gamers have been encouraged to boycott conventions such as the Penny Arcade Expos (PAX) in order to take a stand against discrimination and harrassment in gaming.

Zoe Quinn decided that the positives outweigh the negatives despite having been driven out of her Toronto home by haters who had gone so far as to brag online about putting dead animals in her mailbox. She refused to let them win. Along with some friends, she created Crash Override, an online support group that teamed with the Online Abuse Prevention Initiative to assist developers and others who are dealing with similar abuse.

At the 2015 Game Developers Conference in San Francisco, Quinn told the crowd that victims of harassment, whether they work in the industry or are gamers, should document everything. She also pointed out that if the emotional stress of going through

WELL, YOU DON'T LOOK LIKE A GAMER..."

Accomplished game designer Elizabeth Sampat does not believe that hoping more women work their way into the industry is enough. She understands, based on GamerGate and the fact that it has been a male-dominated business, that many women have hesitated to join the ranks.

So Sampat urges women to urge other women to pursue their dreams. She has expressed her feeling that recruitment is necessary, even of those who have yet to show a lifelong dedication to the field. She has also voiced her view in no uncertain terms in a blog post for the game site Gamasutra, writing the following:

> If you yourself are a woman, be vocal to friends in tech and outside of the industry in general about what you do and why you love it. If you represent a company, sponsor game jams for people who have never made games before. When you're in an interview, quit looking for lifelong dedication and start looking for curiosity and current interest.

Sampat went on to explain that it took urging from her friends to pursue a career in game design.

all the hate messages proves overwhelming, a friend should be summoned to do it instead.

At one point, Quinn's life was in shambles. But she had the courage to continue a game-developing career she loved despite carrying with her an intense anger at those who placed any blame for GamerGate on her. "I'm losing patience with people who say, 'maybe the truth is somewhere in the middle,'" she told the *Guardian*. "Really? Who sees somebody burning down a house and says, 'maybe we should get the arsonist's opinion?'"

Quinn is far from the only woman in the industry who has come to the rescue of her peers. Another is game designer and activist Elizabeth Sampat. Sampat helped Quinn deal with her struggles after receiving abuse herself for urging those who have experienced harassment to stop attending Penny Arcade Expos (PAX), where gamers converge to compete. Sampat has stated that some victims decline to make their voices heard because they don't feel their problems warrant attention. She urged every victim to speak up.

Among those who did speak up was Neha Nair, who toiled in the user relations department with mobile game publisher Storm8. Nair was picked on unmercifully for her Indian heritage and weight. She was glad that she eventually did seek help.

"I was attacked as a woman and a lot for my race," Nair said during a panel discussion at the San Francisco event. "I would read these comments and sit in my room and cry...Don't be embarrassed. Don't be afraid. Too many dreams slip away...I am my own knight. You will have all of these negative comments. Don't let it bring you down."

One might argue that this is easier said than done in an atmosphere that can be toxic. But the point being made is that one cannot allow the haters to win. Had they driven Quinn or Nair

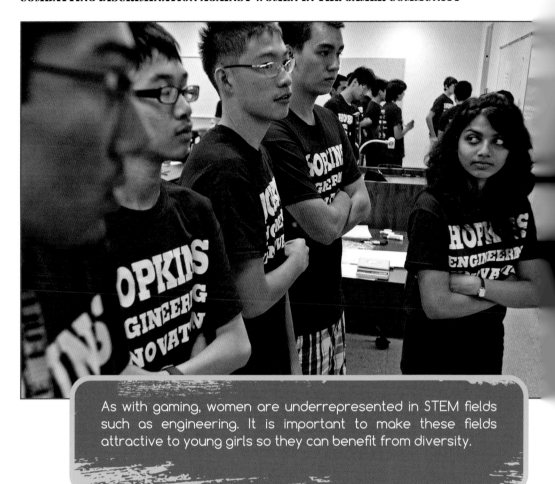

As with gaming, women are underrepresented in STEM fields such as engineering. It is important to make these fields attractive to young girls so they can benefit from diversity.

out of the business, they could have declared victory. It is the haters that need to be silenced rather than those simply trying to make a living.

The stories from such women as Quinn, Sampat, and Nair were all a bit different, but their messages are the same to victims of harassment both inside and outside the industry. That is, there is support out there for one and all. Nobody should suffer anymore. The time had arrived to fight back and make certain that any female who yearns to live out her dream in the gaming industry must no longer face unfair obstacles along the way.

HATERS AND GAMERS

The first glance at the results of a survey conducted in 2014 by the highly respected Pew Research Center is an eye-opening experience. It screams out the fact that female gamers feel shunned and discriminated against by online gaming sites.

The following question was asked: How welcoming are online "neighborhoods" to men and women? The five categories selected included gaming sites, dating sites, social networking, website comment sections, and discussion sites. In the last four categories combined, 50 percent believed women were more welcome, while 44 percent gave the nod to men. In those categories, a vast majority believed the neighborhoods were equally welcome.

But online gaming? A whopping 44 percent believe men are more welcome while just 3 percent consider women more welcome. (Fifty-one percent believe men and women are equally welcome.) The difference is stunning. Many female gamers simply do not feel comfortable on online sites.

They certainly feel comfortable playing video games. A study by the Entertainment Software Association revealed that adult women make up the largest segment of the game-playing population. Women older than eighteen make up 36 percent of the entire gamer community while teenage boys under eighteen make up 17 percent. The number of female gamers age fifty and older rose a whopping 32 percent from 2012 to 2013 alone.

Many women believe they are better off, however, merely playing in the comfort of their own homes against friends and family members. Online gaming in multiplayer settings threatens intimidation, insults, and even physical harm from trolls. Websites such as Not in the Kitchen Anymore and Fat, Ugly or Slutty have allowed female gamers to post and reply to a myriad of disgusting messages from their male counterparts, from sexual propositions to death threats.

Both sites are replete with obscenity-laced recordings and posts, mostly coming from the mouths and keyboards of young men. One called a female gamer a "frickin' stupid skank." Another stated that his opponent was a "slut." Yet another encouraged a gaming foe to "go have some naughty dreams about [boy band] NSYNC or whatever turns you lil nerdy girls on nowadays." And those were among the kinder posts. Many of the others were far more profane.

Women who detail such revolting conversations with haters embrace the opportunity on such supportive sites. It allows them to reveal that their complaints that have been dismissed by some in the past have merit. They are thankful that sites such as Not in the Kitchen Anymore and Fat, Ugly or Slutty have given them a forum to vent their anger and place a spotlight on the repulsive trolling that has become commonplace over the years.

Those who have been abused on online gaming sites might believe that all the nasty posts are written by miserable people. Although some certainly are, others have been inflicted with what has been described as "online disinhibition effect," which was coined by psychologist John Suller. One of the most blatant and horrific examples occurred in 2011, when a Pennsylvania man was jailed after taking over a Facebook tribute page to a fourteen-year-old girl who had committed suicide. He wrote crass jokes and insults despite never having met the girl in person.

Such a case is extreme, but it explains the disinhibition of trolls who deliver disgusting messages to female gamers. They feel free to be rude and aggressive online because the lack of face-to-face contact results in less empathy for others and the

Online communities more easily enable socially unacceptable behavior because activity is anonymous. Those men who harrass and shame women online most likely would not have the courage to do it face-to-face.

attitude that they can get away with anything. As posters hiding behind the anonymity of a user name, there are no consequences of their actions other than a possible insult in return.

Suller explored these factors and others, including the sense that what happens online is not real life. After all, if one hurls insulting profanity at another in person, he or she risks a sock in the nose. But there is no risk of a physical confrontation on a gaming site, so trolls see a green light to express any disgusting thought that comes to mind. And disgusting thoughts indeed pop into the heads of some men whose male egos have been bruised by their defeat in a game by a female.

"There is a feature of the online world that makes such negative behavior more likely than in the real world," said Internet psychologist Graham Jones. "In the real world people subconsciously monitor the behavior of others around them and adapt their own behavior accordingly…Online we do not have such feedback mechanisms."

Feedback mechanisms include body language and facial expressions. A study conducted at the University of Haifa revealed that people forced to make eye contact were half as likely to be hostile than those who were not.

Harder to Be Nice Online?

Though women gamers who have received insults and threats will likely never perceive online disinhibition effect as an excuse, it does provide a bit of an understanding as to why trolls feel like they have the license to behave so terribly. Those who communicate online have a responsibility unlike people in previous generations. If it is indeed more difficult to control negative emotions in a new era of limited human contact, people must work harder to be nice to others online.

NOT JUST
TEENAGE TROLLS

The creation of her documentary *GTFO* was an eye-opening experience for filmmaker Shannon Sun-Higginson. One discovery that surprised her was that the online haters who had been harassing women gamers were not all teenagers. She had believed that immaturity was a driving force to trolling but learned differently.

"I was definitely surprised by how many of them were adults," she told *Time* magazine online. "When you think of people saying really obscene things online, you think it's a teenager. Hearing those adult male voices was pretty shocking."

Sun-Higginson did not meet any of those men in person and refused to give them the publicity they might have been seeking by being included in her film.

Those who aren't nice to women gamers were targeted in a 2015 American documentary titled *GTFO: Get the F&#% Out*. It was directed by New York City filmmaker Shannon Sun-Higginson, who was inspired to create the film after watching a video clip from the live-stream gaming reality show competition *Cross Assault* in which a male player repeatedly sexually harassed his female teammate. Sun-Higginson explored both the positive and negative aspects of women in gaming.

The documentary gave a voice to female gamers who have become familiar with such abuse. Those who had not shared their experiences with others certainly knew after watching the film that they were not alone. It featured interviews with players, developers, and journalists delving into how common sexist behavior had become in the world of gaming.

Women quoted in *GTFO* spoke about threats of rape and murder as if they were everyday occurrences. Former BioWare game writer Jennifer Brandes Hepler claimed she was receiving five hundred harassing e-mails per day, including one in which

This man seems fine with losing to a woman, but other men do not take kindly to being defeated by female gamers. This injury to the ego can result in insulting and threatening messages on online sites.

the writer threatened to kill her children. One rather creepy scene in the film shows a male gamer smelling the hair of a female counterpart during a tournament.

The documentary did not give a completely pessimistic view of the future of gaming as it relates to male-female relationships. It left the impression that the gaming world is in a perpetual state of maturation. In researching her subject matter, Sun-Higginson gained tremendous respect for the women she featured, particularly those still trying to make a living in the business.

"If you're a woman in gaming and you watch this movie, what would be the take away?" she asked. "I guess what we decided upon was that the women who are in this movie and are still in the industry—women who have received threats—are incredibly strong and impressive people."

Thanks to support sites such as Not in the Kitchen Anymore and Fat, Ugly or Slutty, incredibly strong and impressive gamers have a place to turn when they, too, have been victimized. The realization that they are not alone and that there is understanding from other women is of great comfort. So is the knowledge that the haters make up only a small percentage of male gamers, most of whom are empathetic and respectful.

Indeed, things are changing for the better. More women are playing video games than ever before. Game manufacturers are hiring more women. Game developers have created more female protagonists in less sexualized shapes and outfits. In addition, online sites have given women an outlet to expose trolls and vent their anger and frustration. The gaming world has taken a glimpse into the future.

CHAPTER FIVE

A BRIGHTER
TOMORROW

People can learn from their mistakes. So can huge corporations. Tech giant Intel, which manufactures video games, certainly did after playing a dubious role in the GamerGate controversy.

In the fall of 2014, the company succumbed to pressure and removed its advertising from Gamasutra, a website that ran a column supporting women in the gaming community and shed light on the negative portrayals of women in video games themselves. Intel yanked its ads without realizing it was playing into the hands of those accused of harassing women.

Intel apologized and restored the ads on Gamasutra, but its reputation had been damaged. It has since worked diligently to right its wrongs. In early 2015, it announced that it had launched a massive diversity program that required a $300 million investment over five years. Its stated intention was to create a workforce that reflected the American population. "It's good business and it's the right thing to do," exclaimed Intel chief executive Brian Krzanich.

Krzanich admitted the task would not be easy. It would mean plenty of time and money put into tech education for women and minorities. But then, few worthwhile endeavors in life are easy, as female gamers and women in the gaming industry who have overcome or are working to overcome victimization can attest.

The diversification of Intel could have a positive mushrooming effect. It could lead to other tech companies hiring more women. That could lead to the creation of a higher percentage of less sexualized female protagonists in games. That, in turn, could lead to a greater appreciation of positive female imagery for both young male and female gamers, which could lead to a healthier perception of women among the male population. And that could lead to a better relationship between the two sexes online.

Until that ultimate goal is reached, female gamers must understand all their options and realize that the decisions they make are personal and should reflect what is best for them. It is easy for others to say they should be strong enough to stand up to the abuse of online trolls. But for some who are more sensitive than others or to whom online gaming might not be worth the trouble, there is always the simple pleasure of playing video games with only friends and family in the comforts of home.

That option does not suffice for gamers who enjoy multiplayer competition and sharing their experiences online. It is their right to continue their pursuits without intimidation or insults. So women who face such harassment must decide on the tact that best suits them. They can match insult with insult and threat with threat. But rather than scare off the haters, that can often serve to embolden them and motivate them to follow through with a harmful act.

There are more palatable choices. The first might be to reason with the troll. Rather than react angrily or defensively, one

DON'T FEED THE TROLLS?

Computer software professional Randi Harper was one of many female victims of online abuse. So she took action. She created the Online Abuse Prevention Initiative, which works to reduce such abuse through analysis and to cooperate efforts.

One debate Harper has tackled is whether it is best to respond to trolls with silence or to take action to stop the harassment. She has offered her opinion at the annual O'Reilly Open Source Convention, which features discussions on such issues.

Harper realized through her own victimization and watching many women getting bullied out of their jobs that she personally could not be silent. She became vocal about online abuse, which in turn made her more of a target for harassment. Despite those experiences, she does not believe silence is golden in regard to fighting the haters.

"'Don't feed the trolls' has often been said to be a silencing mechanism, but I don't really think that's true," Harper said.

might simply ask why he is expressing such horrible thoughts. Bringing a sensitive, human element to an online exchange could sensitize an individual and result in an apology or at least a change in attitude. Many believe that, just like in any conflict in life, it is better to defuse a potentially frightening situation than heighten it.

The failure of that strategy does not leave women without palatable options. Support sites like Crash Override, Not in the Kitchen Anymore, and Fat, Ugly or Slutty have brought some comfort and an outlet for voicing anger and frustration

The notion of feeding the anger of online trolls who disparage women has been rejected by some in favor of simply ignoring them or trying to reason with them.

while exposing trolls for expressing hatred and sexism, often because they simply lost a game to a woman. The Online Abuse Prevention Initiative is also available for those who wish to report mistreatment.

There is strength in numbers. Friendships forged on such sites can provide victims of online intimidation a far greater feeling of security. Women should be encouraged to work together. In eight words, Zoe Quinn summed up the growing feeling among persecuted female gamers when she exclaimed, "Games are awesome. Stop letting jerks hijack them."

Starting gaming clubs at school is one way to build a positive community. Sensitive teachers and advisors can help foster a love of gaming and encourage girls and boys to respect one another.

What is most important, however, is one's own mental and emotional health. Support sites can certainly help, but so can trusted friends, coworkers, and family members. Threats or even mere insults from unseen sources online can cause distress that should not be internalized. The calming effect and benefits of advice from others in one's life should not be underestimated or underappreciated.

Teenagers and young women have other options, such as teachers and guidance counselors, many of whom can be confided in and can be quite helpful. Though the issue of online intimidation might not fall under the category of typical problems expressed by students, one of their responsibilities is to solve issues, and most take it quite seriously.

Though the message Quinn delivered was appropriate for any video game player who extends her experiences online, her words were spoken to game developers. After all, they too have been the target of discrimination. The GamerGate controversy drove some out of the business, but it emboldened others like Quinn to strengthen female presence in the industry.

The result has given women already in the business or seeking a career in gaming hope for the future. Women such as Quinn, Sarkeesian, Sampat, Wu, and Nair have blazed a trail for all to follow. They have spoken out against discrimination and for greater diversity in the workplace. Their courage and dedication have opened the door for other women, and their hope is that those who yearn to step through that door will do so enthusiastically and without fear.

They understand that there is much work to be done, particularly in regard to the perception of women both in real life and in video games themselves. Despite recent progress, it remains true that games created by men for a male audience receive a stronger marketing push than games developed by

A STEP IN THE RIGHT DIRECTION

Several promising games have been released recently that appear to prove that gaming executives are finally paying attention. *Horizon Zero Dawn* and *ReCore*, particularly if they are successful in sales, may mean a marked shift in content offered by top gaming companies. These games feature females who are not characterized by their sexuality, according to the *New York Times*.

The game *Dishonored 2*, for example, features a heroic female character named Emily Kaldwin. In creating Emily, Harvey Smith asked himself, "Is she a character you'd like to be?" If more creators and executives continue to think this way, it seems the growing number of women gamers will have more options when choosing games. And positive portrayals of women may change the minds of many male players, when they consider what it means to be a woman.

women. It also remains true that female protagonists in games pale in number to their male counterparts.

A higher percentage of female game developers can result in ending negative stereotyping. They are more likely to create

The increasing number of women in the gaming industry has resulted in positive changes in regard to depictions of women in the games themselves.

positive imagery and characterizations of women, whether as action heroes or in more staid games. Meanwhile, the hiring of more women on the business side of gaming could mean more money spent on marketing games created by women with less sexualized female protagonists.

This is not to indicate that men are incapable or unwilling to create games with respectable heroes of the opposite sex. The need for more has certainly been determined. But perhaps it will take more women developers and business specialists proving the financial potential of such games to convince men that it is a worthy endeavor.

Sometimes it is best to play video games against those with whom one is comfortable, such as these two teenage friends, rather than against potential online trolls.

Women in the gaming industry have a far more significant problem than female gamers that have been insulted or threatened. The latter can choose to remove themselves from online sites and compete with others with whom they are comfortable and familiar. Professionals would be hard-pressed to simply give up their careers because of gender discrimination. That must be considered by those planning to make gaming their livelihood.

However, times have changed for the better. The push by Intel to create more opportunities for women in all aspects of its business is just one example. The awareness brought to the plight of women by GamerGate has played a role in doubling the percentage of female game developers in a short period of time. That number appears destined to rise. GamerGate has also raised consciousness about the mistreatment of women within the business.

That growing awareness and the support systems both inside and outside the gaming industry allow women gamers and professionals to forge their own paths and pursue their dreams. Things are looking up. And that's good news for men and women alike because Quinn is right: Games are awesome, and a few jerks cannot be allowed to ruin the fun for everyone else.

GLOSSARY

CENSORSHIP Suppressing material deemed inappropriate.

CHARACTERIZATION Portrayal of a fictitious person.

DEMEANING Describes a degrading task or representation.

DEPICTION The representation of a person or event through an image.

DISINHIBITION A feeling of freedom to do whatever one likes.

DOXXING A slang word for publishing the personal information of another individual.

FEMINIST Person who actively supports issues dealing with women's rights and equality.

GAMING The act of participating in computer or video games.

HEROINE A female hero.

IMPERSONATE Pretending to be another person through voice or action.

INTERACTIVE Relating to someone else through personal or electronic communication.

MARKETING The promotion of a person or product in an attempt to earn money.

MISOGYNIST A person who dislikes or mistreats women.

OBJECTIFICATION To present a person as an object rather than someone with emotional or mental qualities.

OBSCENITY A swear word or dirty act.

PARANOID To be unduly worried or frightened.

PERSECUTION The act of harassing someone, most often for his or her gender, race, or religion.

PROTAGONIST The lead character or hero.

STEREOTYPING A simplified conception or image of a person or group.

SUBORDINATE A person in relation to his or her boss in a business.

TROLL An annoying or threatening online presence.

VICTIMIZE To make a victim of another person.

Amnesty International USA
5 Penn Place
New York, NY 10001
(212) 807-8400
Website: http://www.amnestyusa.org/our-work/issues/
    women-s-rights/violence-against-women
Among other tasks, this organization works to end violence
    against women worldwide.

Entertainment Software Association of Canada (ESAC)
130 Spadina Avenue, Suite 408
Toronto, ON M5V 2L4
Canada
(416) 620-7171
Website: http://theesa.ca
The ESAC works to ensure that Canada remains a great place
    to create and publish video games.

Games for Change
205 E. 42nd Street, 20th Floor
New York, NY 10017
(212) 242-4922
Website: http://www.gamesforchange.org
This group works to create and distribute social impact games
    that serve to aid in humanitarian and educational efforts.

Global Gaming Women
799 9th Street NW, Suite 700
Washington, DC 20001

(202) 552-2675
Website: http://www.globalgamingwomen.org
As part of the American Gaming Association, the aim of this
    group is to support women in the international gaming
    industry through education, mentorship, and networking
    opportunities.

Live Your Dream
1709 Spruce Street
Philadelphia, PA 19103
(215) 893-9000
Website: http://www.liveyourdream.org
This online volunteer network works to support women and
    girls in their quest to lead better lives.

National Domestic Violence Hotline
P.O. Box 161810
Austin, TX 78716
(800) 799-7233
Website: http://www.thehotline.org
This hotline not only provides help to those in immediate
    need but gives advice to those seeking guidance on how
    to aid someone they know.

National Organization for Women (NOW)
1100 H Street NW, Suite 300
Washington, DC 20005
(202) 628-8669
Website: http://now.org
NOW deals with a myriad of issues concerning women,
    including the battle to end violence against women.

Soroptimist
1709 Spruce Street
Philadelphia, PA 19103
(215) 893-9000
Website: http://www.soroptimist.org
This global women's organization runs programs to bring
social and economic empowerment to women and girls.

Women Abuse Council of Toronto
1652 Keele Street, Suite 129
Toronto, ON M6M 3W3
Canada
(416) 944-9242
Website: http://www.womanabuse.ca
This organization develops policy and improves services for
assaulted women and their families.

Women in Games International
Website: http://www.womeningamesinternational.org
This organization made up of professionals of both sexes in
the global gaming industry works to promote inclusion of
women in the business.

Websites

Because of the changing nature of Internet links, Rosen Publishing
has developed an online list of websites related to the subject of
this book. This site is updated regularly. Please use this link to
access this list:

http://www.rosenlinks.com/CSTC/gamer

Brathwaite, Brenda, and Ian Schreiber. *Breaking into the Game Industry: Advice for a Successful Career from Those Who Have Done It.* Boston, MA: Cengage Learning, 2011.

Guinness World Records. *Guinness World Records 2016 Gamer's Edition.* London, U.K.: Guinness World Records, 2015.

Jacobs, Thomas A. *Teen Cyberbullying Investigated: Where Do Your Rights End and Consequences Begin?* Golden Valley, MN: Free Spirit Publishing, 2010.

Janason. *Stop the Cyberbullies and Internet Trolls Once and For All.* Amazon Digital Services, 2015.

Kowalski, Robin M., Susan P. Limber, and Patricia W Agataston. *Cyberbullying: Bullying in the Digital Age.* Hoboken, NJ: Wiley-Blackwell, 2012.

Parkin, Simon. *An Illustrated History of 151 Video Games.* London, U.K.: Lorenz Books, 2014.

Patchin, Justin W., and Sameer Hinduja. *Bullying Beyond the Schoolyard: Preventing and Responding to Cyberbullying.* New York, NY: Crown Publishing, 2014.

Patchin, Justin W., and Sameer Hinduja. *Words Wound: Delete Cyberbullying and Make Kindness Go Viral.* Golden Valley, MN: Free Spirit Publishing, 2013.

Rogers, Scott. *Level Up! The Guide to Great Video Game Design.* Hoboken, NJ: John Wiley & Sons, 2010.

Schell, Jesse. *The Art of Game Design: A Book of Lenses.* Boca Raton, FL: CRC Press, 2014.

Shore, Kenneth: *The ABCs of Bullying Prevention.* Naples, FL: National Professional Resources/Dude Publishing, 2011.

Skolnick, Evan. *Video Game Storytelling: What Every Developer Needs to Know About Narrative Techniques.* New York, NY: Watson-Guptill, 2014.

Todd, Paula. *Extreme Mean: Trolls, Bullies, and Predators Online.* Oxford, U.K.: 2014.

BIBLIOGRAPHY

Feminist Frequency: YouTube. "Damsel in Distress: Part 2
    – Tropes vs. Women in Video Games." Retrieved
    December 10, 2015 (https://www.youtube.com/
    watch?v=toa_vH6xGqs).

Isaacson, Betsy. "#1ReasonWhy Reveals Sexism Rampant in
    the Gaming Industry." *Huffington Post*, November 29,
    2012. Retrieved December 9, 2015 (http://www
    .huffingtonpost.com/2012/11/29/1reasonwhy-reveals
    -sexism-gaming-industry_n_2205204.html).

Kleeman, Sophie. "5 Charts That Show Sexism Is Still Alive
    and Well in Gaming." Mic.com, June 30, 2015. Retrieved
    December 14, 2015 (http://mic.com/articles/121528/sexism
    -in-gaming#.IEvhy5GK6).

Makuch, Eddie. "Percentage of Female Developers Has More
    Than Doubled Since 2009." GameSpot, June 24, 2014.
    Retrieved December 19, 2015 (http://www.gamespot.com/
    articles/percentage-of-female-developers-has-more-than
    -doubled-since-2009/1100-6420680).

Mantilla, Karla. *Gendertrolling: How Misogyny Went Viral.*
    Santa Barbara, CA: Praeger, 2015.

Martens, Todd. "SXSW: Female Gamers Tell Their Stories in
    'GTFO,' Which Tackles Industry Sexism." *Los Angeles
    Times*, March 13, 2015. Retrieved December 20, 2015

(http://herocomplex.latimes.com/games/female-gamers -tell-their-stories-in-gtfo-which-tackles-sexism-in-gaming -industry).

Martin, Alan. "Online Disinhibition and the Psychology of Trolling." *Wired*, May 30, 2013. Retrieved December 18, 2015 (http://www.wired.co.uk/news/archive/2013-05/30/ online-aggression).

National Coalition Against Domestic Violence. "National Statistics." Retrieved December 17, 2015 (http://www .ncadv.org/learn/statistics).

Porter, Justin. "Lara Croft Has Company: More Female Heroes Appear in Big-Budget Games." *The New York Times*, December 28, 2015. Retrieved January 5, 2015 (http:// www.nytimes.com/2015/12/29/arts/lara-croft-has -company-more-female-heroes-appear-in-big-budget -games.html?smid=nytcore-iphone-share&smprod= nytcore-iphone&_r=0.)

Santayarayana, Megha. "Video Game Industry Stung by Stigma of Objectifying Women." TribLive, September 4, 2014. Retrieved December 8, 2015 (http://triblive.com/news/ allegheny/6728585-74/games-video-game#axzz3uP7wig4l).

Stermer, Steven Paul, and Stephen R. Burgess, "Sex, Lies, and Video Games: The Portrayal of Male and Female Characters on Video Game Covers." *Sex Roles*, September 2007. Retrieved December 12, 2015 (http://link.springer .com/article/10.1007%2Fs11199-007-9250-0).

Sullivan, Gail. "Study: More Women Than Teenage Boys Are Gamers." *The Washington Post*, August 22, 2014. Retrieved December 16, 2015 (https://www.washington post.com/news/morning-mix/wp/2014/08/22/adult-women -gamers-outnumber-teenage-boys).

Takahashi, Dean. "Intel Turns Its GamerGate Gaffe into a Huge Pro-Diversity Program." VentureBeat, January 6, 2015. Retrieved December 16, 2015 (http://venturebeat. com/2015/01/06/intel-turns-its-gamergate-gaffe-into -a-huge-pro-diversity-program).

Takahashi, Dean. "Zoe Quinn and Other Female Game Developers Speak Out Against Harassment." VentureBeat, March 4, 2015. Retrieved December 18, 2015 (http://venturebeat.com/2015/03/04/zoe-quinn -and-other-female-game-developers-speak-out -against-harassment).

Totilo, Stephen. "And Here's Why Women in the Games Business Put Up with So Much Crap." *Kotaku*, November 27, 2012. Retrieved December 10, 2015 (http://kotaku .com/5963755/and-heres-why-women-in-the-games -business-put-up-with-so-much-crap).

Wingfield, Nick. "Feminist Critics of Video Games Facing Threats in 'GamerGate' Campaign." *The New York Times*, October 16, 2014. Retrieved December 9, 2015 (http:// www.nytimes.com/2014/10/16/technology/gamergate -women-video-game-threats-anita-sarkeesian.html).

Yao, Mike Z., Chad Mahood, and Daniel Linz. "Sexual Priming, Gender Stereotyping, and Likelihood to Sexually Harass: Examining the Cognitive Effects of Playing a Sexually-Explicit Video Game." *Sex Roles*, January 2010. Retrieved December 19, 2015 (http://link.springer.com/article/10.1007/s11199-009-9695-4/fulltext.html).

INDEX

About the Author

Martin Gitlin is a writer and author based in Cleveland, Ohio. He has had more than one hundred educational books published since 2006, including many in the realms of social studies and pop culture. During his eleven years in the newspaper industry, he won more than forty-five writing awards, including first place for general excellence from the Associated Press.

Photo Credits